# Letterland

# First Picture Word Book

Designed by Susi Martin and Lisa MacLeod

Illustrated by Geri Livingston Studio and Ainslie MacLeod

Based on original characters designed by Lyn Wendon

# Welcome to Letterland

## About Letterland

**Letterland is an imaginary place where letters come to life! The friendly Letterland characters help children to easily understand the sound and shape of letters – one of the key skills needed when learning to read and write.**

Simple stories about the Letterland characters explain letter sounds and shapes, so that confusion over similar looking letters is avoided and children are motivated to listen, think and learn.

One of Letterland's keys to success is its 'Sound Trick'. By just starting to pronounce a character's name, such as 'a...' (Annie Apple), 'b...' (Bouncy Ben), 'c...' (Clever Cat), a child automatically says the correct letter sound. It's that simple! The combination of memorable characters and proven educational principles makes Letterland the ideal way to introduce your child to the alphabet.

For more information, including a pronunciation guide for all the letter sounds, see: **www.letterland.com**

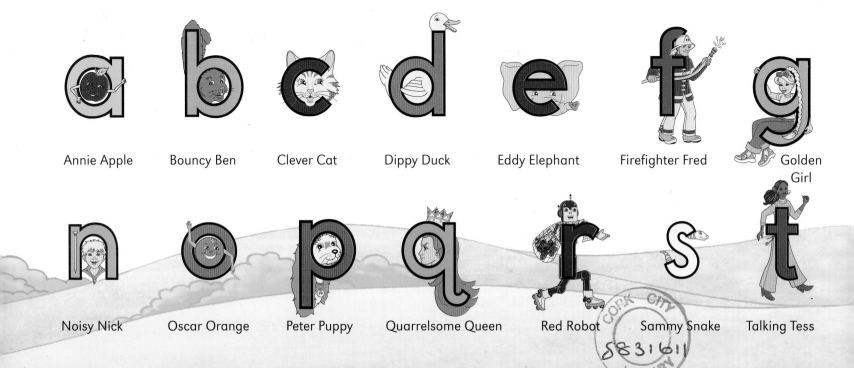

Annie Apple    Bouncy Ben    Clever Cat    Dippy Duck    Eddy Elephant    Firefighter Fred    Golden Girl

Noisy Nick    Oscar Orange    Peter Puppy    Quarrelsome Queen    Red Robot    Sammy Snake    Talking Tess

# About this book

Here are some ways you can enjoy the *First Picture Word Book* with your child.

- Look at the words together and, as you say each one, point to the first letter. Say the Letterlanders' names together. Remember, just by starting to say a Letterlander's name, for example, 'fff...' for Firefighter Fred, children will automatically be making the sound they will need for reading.

- Encourage children to name the pictures and point at the words as they do so. Soon they will realise that they are reading!

- Find the same Letterlander in each scene. Look for things that begin with that character's sound and talk about them.

- Try making up stories together about what the Letterlanders could be doing with the objects on their page. Think about other words that start with the same letter. Talk about what Munching Mike might like to eat – mushrooms, marmite or macaroni? Or what pets Harry Hat Man might have – a horse, hamster or hedgehog?

- When you are out and about together, look for some of the words that you have seen in this book, such as 'EXIT' or 'sandwich' or 'up'.

Harry Hat Man    Impy Ink    Jumping Jim    Kicking King    Lucy Lamp Light    Munching Mike

Uppy Umbrella    Vicky Violet    Walter Walrus    Fix-it Max    Yellow Yo-yo Man    Zig Zag Zebra

**Aa**

astronaut

apples

anteater

ant

alligator

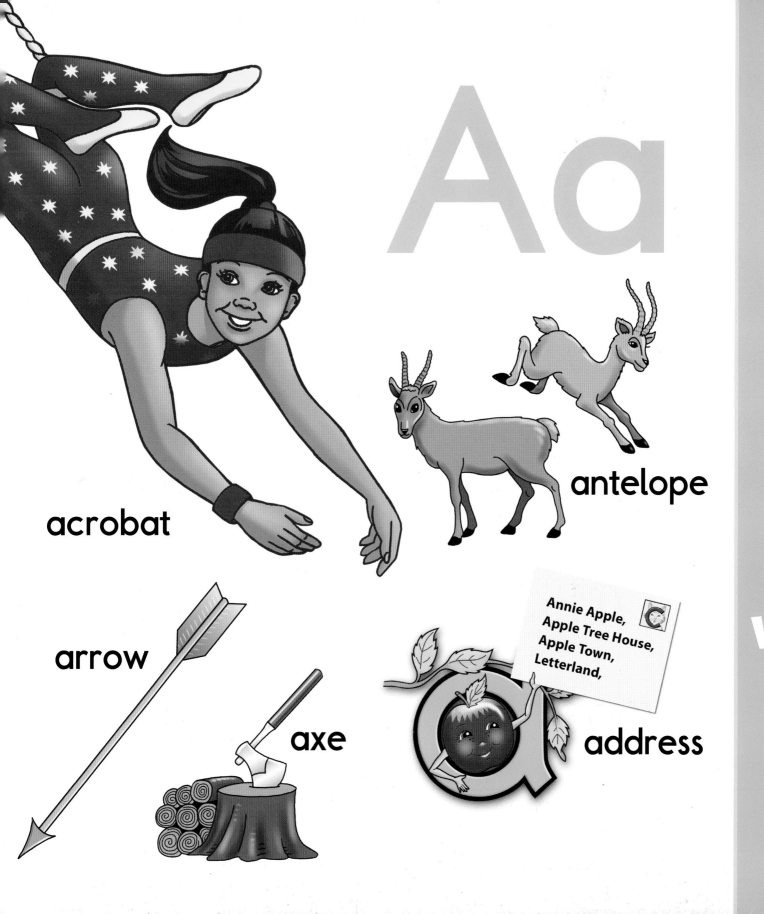

# Aa

acrobat

antelope

arrow

axe

address

Annie Apple,
Apple Tree House,
Apple Town,
Letterland,

**Bb**

balloon

boy

butterfly

bird

ball

boat

## Bb

books

bat

bicycle

buttercups

bees

Nn
Oo
Pp
Qq
Rr
Ss
Tt
Uu
Vv
Ww
Xx
Yy
Zz

Aa
Bb
Cc
Dd
Ee
Ff
Gg
Hh
Ii
Jj
Kk
Ll
Mm

Cc

cake

cat

castle

cow

caterpillar

car

# Cc

crab

clock

clown

cup

# Dd

donkey

dog

drum

dinosaur

daisies

dolphin

doll

dragonflies

daffodils

# Dd

Nn
Oo
Pp
Qq
Rr
Ss
Tt
Uu
Vv
Ww
Xx
Yy
Zz

# E e  E e

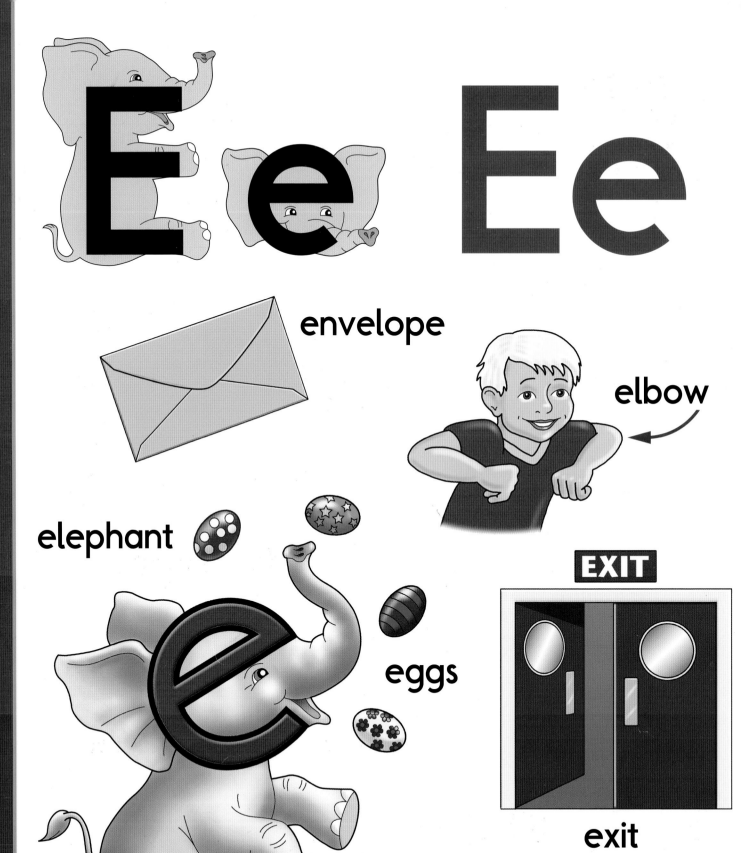

envelope

elbow

elephant

eggs

EXIT

exit

Ff

Ff

flowers

fire engine

frog

fish

fire

Nn
Oo
Pp
Qq
Rr
Ss
Tt
Uu
Vv
Ww
Xx
Yy
Zz

Aa Bb Cc Dd Ee Ff **Gg** Hh Ii Jj Kk Ll Mm

# Gg

girl

goldfish

geese

go-cart

gate

grapes

glasses

gorilla

guitar

goat

# Gg

# Hh

hammer

hens

hat

horse

hay

hands

Hh

hippo

house

hedgehogs

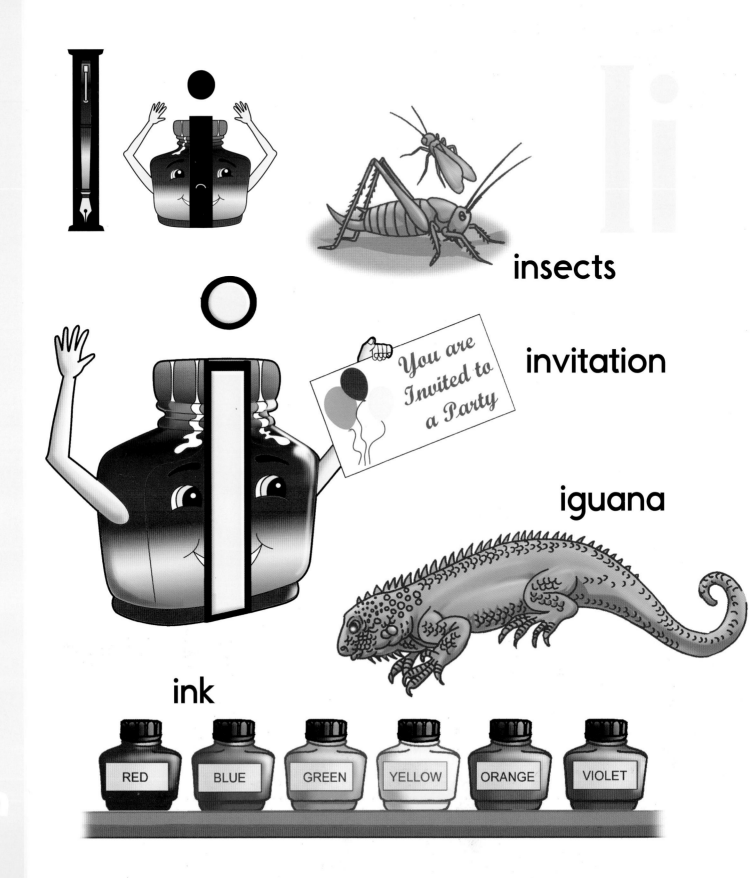

insects

invitation

iguana

ink

RED  BLUE  GREEN  YELLOW  ORANGE  VIOLET

jelly

Jj

jet

jigsaw
puzzle

jeep

juggle

19

kite

king

key

kick

kennel

kettle

# Kk

kitten

kangaroo

koala

Aa
Bb
Cc
Dd
Ee
Ff
Gg
Hh
Ii
Jj
Kk
Ll
Mm

22

lollipop

leaf

leopard

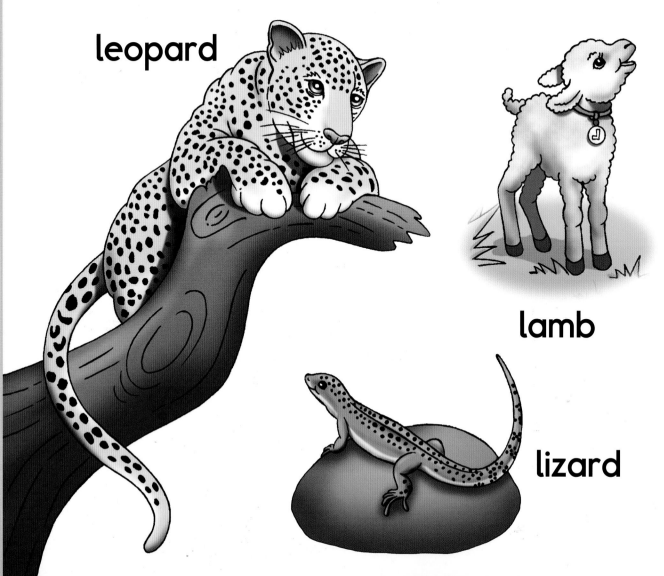

lamb

lizard

lemons

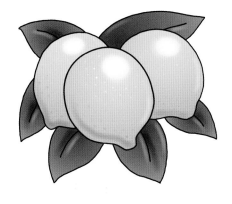

lighthouse

# Ll

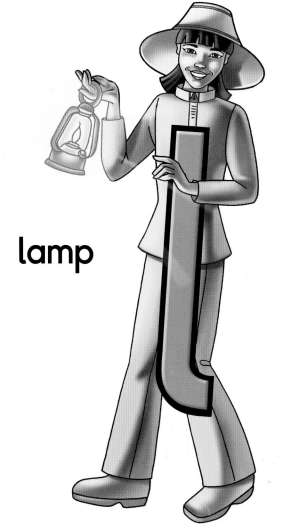

lamp

lion

# Mm

moon

mountains

milk

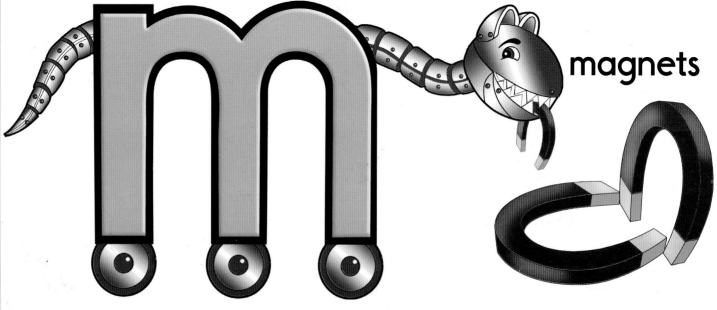

magnets

mouse

# Mm

mushrooms

moth

monkey

mirror

# Nn Nn

nest

night

nails

needle

nuts

oranges

octopus

ostrich

otter

ORANGES

Aa
Bb
Cc
Dd
Ee
Ff
Gg
Hh
Ii
Jj
Kk
Ll
Mm

Pp

pears

pizza

puppy

pond

penguins

plane

# Pp

pencils

parrot

pirate

polar bears

Aa
Bb
Cc
Dd
Ee
Ff
Gg
Hh
Ii
Jj
Kk
Ll
Mm

30

# Qq

quarter

queen

quiz

quilt

quail

# R r

# Rr

rocket

rainbow

roses

robot

rollerskates

Nn
Oo
Pp
Qq
Rr
Ss
Tt
Uu
Vv
Ww
Xx
Yy
Zz

# Ss

seagull

sun shade

sandcastle

sun bed

sandwich

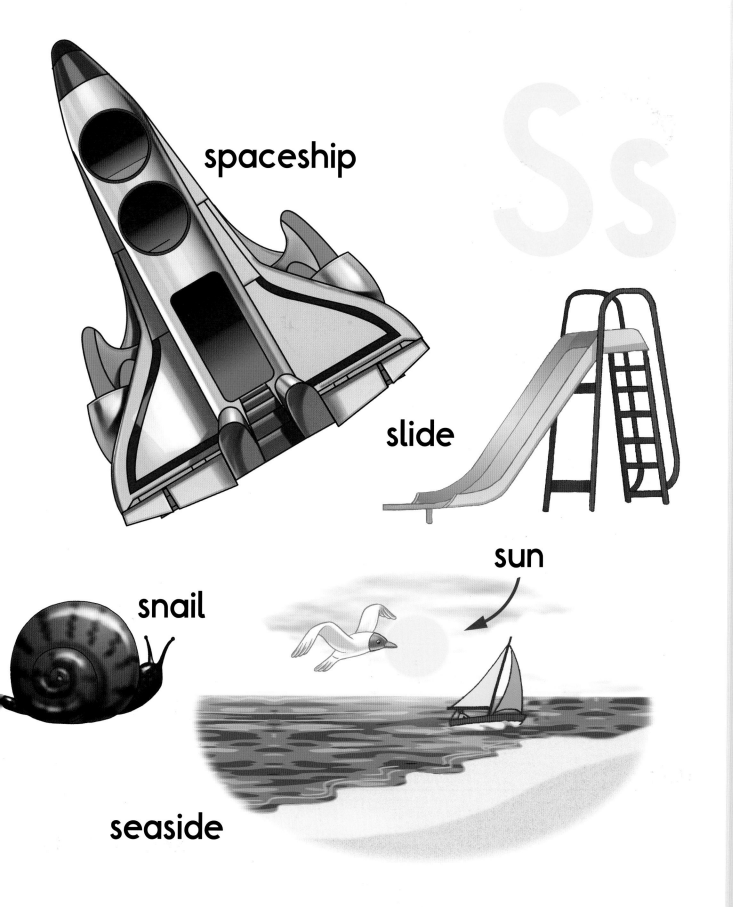

spaceship

slide

sun

snail

seaside

Nn
Oo
Pp
Qq
Rr
Ss
Tt
Uu
Vv
Ww
Xx
Yy
Zz

table

tree

toys

tractor

telescope

**Tt**

teddy bear

tiger

tent

telephone

# Uu Uu

umbrella

upside down

underwater

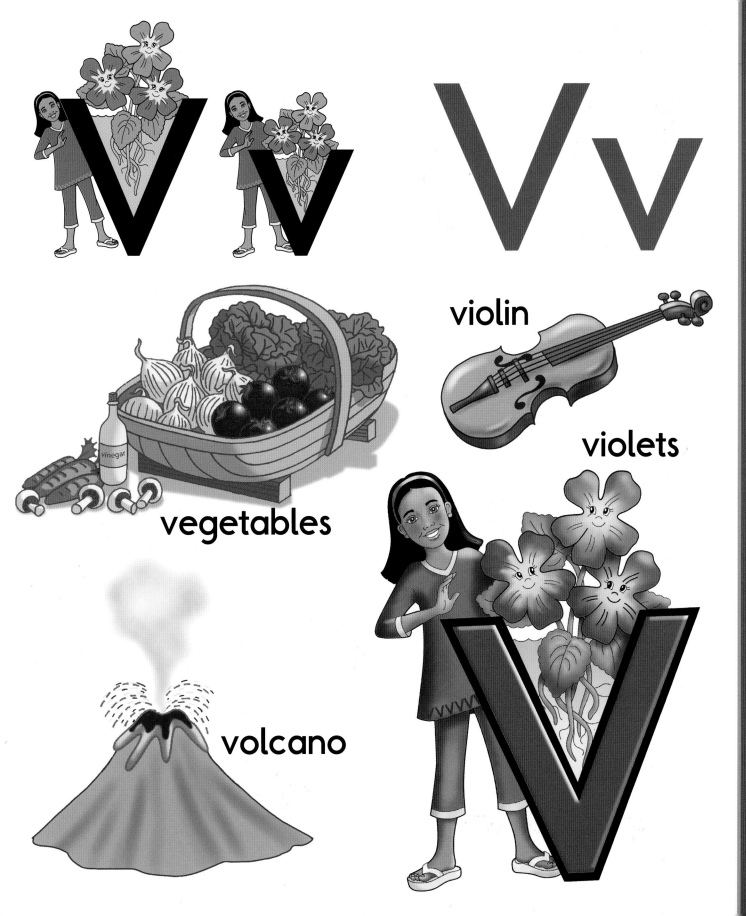

# Vv

violin

violets

vegetables

volcano

Nn
Oo
Pp
Qq
Rr
Ss
Tt
Uu
Vv
Ww
Xx
Yy
Zz

37

W w W w

web

windmill

waterfall

walrus

whale

Xx

fox

box

taxi

fix it

Nn
Oo
Pp
Qq
Rr
Ss
Tt
Uu
Vv
Ww
Xx
Yy
Zz

Aa
Bb
Cc
Dd
Ee
Ff
Gg
Hh
Ii
Jj
Kk
Ll
Mm

yogurt

yacht

yawn

yak

yo-yo

Z z

Zz

zigzag

zip

zoo

zebra

Nn
Oo
Pp
Qq
Rr
Ss
Tt
Uu
Vv
Ww
Xx
Yy
Zz

# Numbers

1 car

2 umbrellas

3 hens

4 books

5 flowers

6 balloons

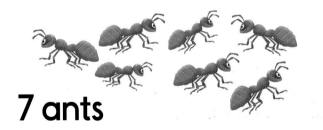

7 ants

8 hats

**9 needles**

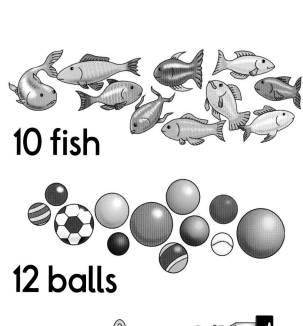
**10 fish**

**11 butterflies**

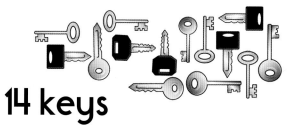
**12 balls**

**13 pencils**

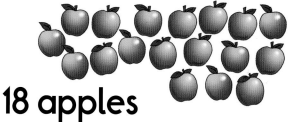
**14 keys**

**15 eggs**

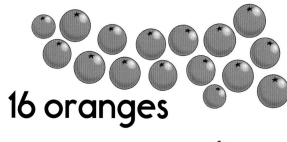
**16 oranges**

**17 carrots**

**18 apples**

**19 cups**

**20 stars**

11
12
13
14
15
16
17
18
19
20

# Colours

**purple butterfly**

**yellow lemons**

**green grapes**

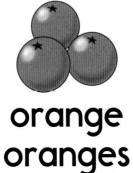

**orange oranges**

**pink flowers**

**red roses**

**black and white zebra**

**blue ball**

# Shapes

triangle

circle

square

rectangle

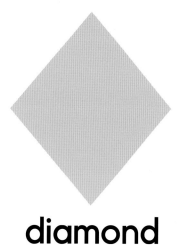
diamond

hexagon

pentagon

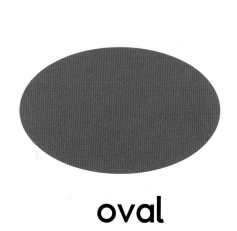
oval

star

# Animals

**sheep**

**chicken**

**cow**

**cat**

**goose**

**horse**

**goat**

**duck**

**dog**

# Letterland

## Child-friendly phonics

The Letterland system teaches all 44 sounds in the English language through stories rather than rules. There are resources to take children from the very first stages of learning to full literacy.

## ABC Trilogy

**ABC**
Story Phonics - making letters come to life!

**Beyond ABC**
New edition
Story Phonics - making letters come to life!

**Far Beyond ABC**
Story Phonics - making letters come to life!

**ABC Activity Book**
Includes stickers
Activities for every letter of the alphabet

**Beyond ABC Activity Book**
Includes 50 reusable stickers
Activities for 19 major spelling patterns

**Far Beyond ABC Activity Book**
Includes 50 reusable stickers
Activities for 18 major spelling patterns

## Sticker & Activity Books

**Cookbook**
An alphabet of recipes

**Things to Make & Do**
An a-z of craft and play ideas

**Fun-to-Find Sticker Book**
Includes 52 reusable stickers
80+ fun things to find and stick on!

**First Sticker Dictionary**
52 fun stickers to help you learn the alphabet

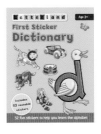
**Harry Hat Man's HOLIDAY Activity Book**
PLUS an a-z of eco-tips for kids... & grown-ups!

**Bouncy Ben's Brain Busters**
An a-z of activities with hours of fun for everyone!

## Picture Books

**Bedtime Stories**
An a-z of illustrated stories

**Alphabet Tales**
An a-z of illustrated stories

**Who's Hiding?**
A lift-the-flap ABC book

**ABC Stories**
Read together, read alone, read aloud!

**Alphabet of Rhymes**
26 vibrant verses from a-z

**First Picture Word Book**
Over 500 words!

**Alphabet Adventures**
Explore and learn from a-z

**Dippy Duck's Day of Discovery**
A journey through the alphabet

## Games & Puzzles

**Giant Alphabet Puzzle**
28 pieces 2 years +

**Dippy Duck's Dance**
singalong squirty bath book

**Sammy Snake's Snap**

**Make-a-Story card game**
Create endless fun sentences!

**Word Cards**
78 cards
Develop reading and spelling skills

**Alphabet Races**
Compete in a Letterland rhyming race and learn your alphabet!

See our full range at: **www.letterland.com**

For product advice and support: **info@letterland.com**

Published by Letterland International Ltd
Leatherhead, Surrey, KT22 9AD, UK

**www.letterland.com**

© Letterland International 2004
10 9 8 7

ISBN: 978-1-86209-244-0
Product Code: T13

First published 1997. This new edition published 2004. Reprinted 2007, 2008, 2010, 2011, 2012, 2014.
LETTERLAND® is a registered trademark of Lyn Wendon.

British Library Cataloguing in Publication Data
A catalogue record for this publication is available from the British Library

Designed by Susi Martin and Lisa MacLeod
Illustrated by the Geri Livingston Studio and Ainslie MacLeod

Printed in China.